Child Abduction

Child Abduction

How To Protect Your Children

Maurice Woodson

Writers Club Press
New York   Lincoln   Shanghai

Child Abduction
How To Protect Your Children

Writers Club Press
an imprint of iUniverse, Inc.

For information address:
iUniverse
2021 Pine Lake Road, Suite 100
Lincoln, NE 68512
www.iuniverse.com

ISBN: 0-595-25360-1 (Pbk)
ISBN: 0-595-65122-4 (Cloth)

Printed in the United States of America

Contents

For Kiana, Anthony, Maya, and all my nieces and nephews.
May your childhoods be wonderful and safe.

Special Thanks to:
All the law enforcement agencies and child protection agencies
that assisted me in the making of this book…especially The
National Center for Missing & Exploited Children. You are
the heros on the frontline of defense in this never ending battle
to protect our children. I thank you and salute you in the
name of all parents.

Introduction

It is a fact that thousands of children are reported missing each year. In the year 2001 alone, police were investigating the disappearances of an astounding 700,000+ children and teens. Not only as a parent of three, but as an uncle and as a cousin to many, this is something that is of major concern to me. There use to be a time when one would have felt secure that their children were in safe havens such as school, church, or day care. Today we realize that even these institutions are not the sacred grounds we thought them to be and that unfortunately neither are our own back or front yards.

One night, while watching the evening news, I was completely devastated. In one broadcast, there were stories of alleged molestation in our schools and in our churches. There were also four other news stories, all of children that were missing or abducted. In two of the stories, the children were actually taken right out of their own homes. What makes it even worse is that there were more abductions going on that never made the evening news. What are we to do as parents? How do we protect our children?

Many of us live in a state of mind whereas we believe that our children are safe and that things like this can only happen to someone else. Unfortunately, the reality is that it can happen to our children. It truly doesn't matter if you live in the city, the suburbs, or the mountains. It doesn't matter if you are rich, poor, or middle income. It certainly doesn't matter what color your skin is or what religion you practice. A child predator can strike anywhere and anytime. This is why it is so important that we educate ourselves and our children. It is also important that we don't just stop there. Once our children are educated, it is our duty and our responsibility to continue to reinforce what we've taught them. It is too important and too dangerous to just assume that they will be prepared in the event that they are approached.

My mother always taught my brothers and me not to talk to strangers and not to accept gifts from people without her direct permission. For the most part, we did as she said, but there was this one time (I don't think she even knows about this) that my brother and I did something that could have left us as story on the evening news.

One day, a man was driving down the street near our home in the Bronx. Seeing my brother and me outside playing, he pulled over and asked us for directions. At the time, my brother was eight and I was ten years old. We knew exactly where this lost man wanted to go, so we leaned into the window and tried to explain it to him. Though the man's destination was only two left turns and one right turn away, he couldn't seem to understand what we were trying to explain to him. What we did next would strike fear into the hearts of any parent (including my mother when she reads this).

My brother and I told this man that we would guide him to where he was going, and without any enticement we proceeded to climb into this stranger's vehicle. We had never seen this man before but we wanted to be helpful. The car drove off with us in the rear and luckily for us this man was exactly what he said he was…lost. He followed our directions to his destination and gave us a dollar apiece and thanked us as we climbed out the car. Without a thought to the seriousness of what we had just done, we each bought a slice of pizza and returned to the playground in front of our building. I think what makes this story even more frightening is that until recently, I never even gave what happened a second thought. This made me begin to wonder if my children are safe and if they truly do know what to do if they are approached. My mother had thought that my brothers and I knew and unfortunately she was wrong.

This book is designed to help guide parents as they educate themselves and their children regarding child abductions. Along with the help and assistance of several police and child protection organizations, I have compiled information and safety tips on what to do to protect your children as well as what to do if your child is abducted. Unfortunately nobody can guarantee the safety of your child, but hopefully with the information you will find in this book (including descriptions of some techniques used by abductors to lure children) and the knowledge of what to look for, then maybe we can prevent our children from becoming the next victims of these predators.

Maurice Woodson

Chapter One

About Abductors

In the movies, it's usually easy to tell who the bad guys are. They usually wear dark clothes, smoke cigarettes, and scowl at everyone. In the real world, unfortunately, there are no distinguishable characteristics. An abductor can be anyone—a nicely dressed stranger, a neighbor, a relative, a friend, a teacher, a delivery man, or even a religious leader.

According to statistics, a child is more likely to be abducted by someone they are familiar with…Someone that they have most likely seen before. However, an abductor can also be a stranger or drifter that happens upon your child—be it at school, at home or at some unpopulated location such as a train yard or a vacant lot. Usually, these predators frequent a location such as a park, a school, or a neighborhood, looking for a target. If they know the target, they will usually follow the child and familiarize themselves with schedules and routines. Whichever the scenario, what they are doing is trying to find an opportunity whereas they can approach or grab an unsuspecting victim (It only takes a moment for them to accomplish their goal).

Below you will find a few of the more common techniques used to lure children. Please note that there as many possible techniques as an imagination can conceive.

The Lost Pet

This technique is used because most children love animals or have a pet of their own. What the predator is trying to do is evoke an emotional desire to want to help find this pet. The predator will show a child a picture of a dog or cat and explain that the animal ran off or got lost. At this point they ask for the child's assistance in locating the animal. After telling the child the pet's name, they ask the child to call out the name of the pet as they lead the child away. This technique is mostly used at parks, beaches, or from front yards of a home or apartment building.

The Injured Parent

This technique is also about evoking an emotional response. The child is approached by the predator and told that their mother or father is injured and that the predator was sent to bring them to their parents. Because children are taught to trust adults, a child would have no reason to doubt the honesty of this person. Also, in most cases, the child is called by name. By hearing their own name, the child feels that the predator must know them, therefore the parents must have sent them. In actuality, the predator probably read the name off a school bag, a toy, a piece of clothing, or heard someone refer to them by name. The goal of the predator here is that the child will probably be so worried about their parents that all that they would be concerned about is getting to them. This technique is mostly used after school.

Lost Stranger

A vehicle pulls up and someone says that they are lost and asks for directions. The goal is to lure the child close enough to the vehicle to grab them or in some cases, to distract them as someone else sneaks up and grabs them. This technique is mostly used at parks, front yards, schools, or while walking home from school or after school activities.

The Frisbee Or Ball Toss

There are a couple of ways that this technique is executed. In one way, an abductor tosses a ball or frisbee toward a child and then asks the child to bring it back to them. When they do, the child is grabbed either by the predator or by an accomplice. In another way, the predator tosses the frisbee or ball past the child. The predator then asks the child to retrieve it for them and when the child complies, an accomplice who has been hiding nearby grabs the child. This is mostly used at parks, beaches, and picnic areas.

The Stop And Grab

The predator notices a child walking alone near the edge of a road or in an unsupervised yard. They drive up as close as possible, jump out of the car, grab the child and then pull off. This can take place anywhere a road runs near or even in a parking lot.

The Family Or Friend Pickup

A family member or acquaintance meets a child who is walking to or from somewhere or who is waiting for a bus. The person then offers to give the child a ride or offers to take them for a snack or some other enticing treat. Once the child is in the car, this person abducts them. In this scenario, the predator is usually an estranged parent, but could be an uncle, a neighbor, a teacher or a religious leader—someone the child would normally trust.

The Friend

This is a patient predator. This person meets their victim several times over a short period. At each meeting, the predator strikes up a conversation with their target, plays with the target, and sometimes even gives the target small gifts or presents. These things are done to gain the trust of the child. During this time, the predator will usually refer to themselves as a "friend" or as a "special friend." Then, one day when the child is unsuspecting, the predator will lead the child away or set them up to be grabbed. This technique can be used at parks, arcades, schools, or anywhere a child may routinely go.

The Mall Snatch

This predator hangs out at a mall or shopping center waiting for an opportunity. They look for a wandering child or for a parent who is preoccupied and not paying close attention to their child. The predator also looks for a parent who sends a child, usually of the opposite sex, into one restroom while they go into the other or while they wait outside. These techniques can be used anywhere there is a crowd-malls, amusement parks, grocery stores, flea markets and street fairs. Beaches, zoos and carnivals are also other areas where this technique is successfully used by predators.

The Home Visitor

This predator is also very patient. In this scenario, the predator usually stakes out a house for a couple of hours to a couple of months. When the predator strikes, they usually approach the target house when they are certain that a child will answer the door. Once the predator reaches the door, they usually have in mind a plan to get the child to unlock the door. Once that happens, the predator snatches the child and can be gone within seconds.

** A REMINDER—These are just a few of the more common techniques used by predators. For more information, contact your local or state police department or NCMEC (The National Center for Missing and Exploited Children).

Chapter Two

How To Talk To And Educate Our Children

As a parent or guardian, It is our responsibility to take every step possible to ensure that our children are safe at all times. Since we cannot be with them every minute of the day, we must educate them on how to be safe.

This chapter will explain and discuss how to talk about news broadcasts dealing with child abductions, safety tips on what a child should do if approached by a "stranger," what to do if lost or separated from a parent or guardian, and how to reinforce what you teach them.

When talking to you children about child abductions, you must tread carefully because you don't want to make a child so afraid that they won't leave the house. Try not to emphasize the frightening details of what might happen to a child who does not follow the safety guidelines. According to child therapists, what you want to do is strike a balance between avoiding the issue and enforcing a sense of fear in your child. The goal is to instill a sense of caution.

In the case of a news broadcast, you should explain what happened using as few gory details as possible. Explain that a child was abducted and that there are some bad people in the world who wish to cause others harm. Use this as an opportunity to reinforce preventive information.

Here are some basic safety tips to teach your child...

* Never go to a friends home without informing your parents where you are going and when you will return.
* Tell parents where you are at all times—leave a written note or leave a recorded message.

* Never talk to strangers.

* Never take candy or gifts from strangers.

* Inform parents of all new friends

* Never wander of when you are with your parents

* If an adult often appears at different locations you go, immediately inform parents and guardians

* move away from any car or vehicle that pulls up next to you, if you do not know the driver.

* Scream and run away from a "stranger" that calls you to a vehicle or attempts to touch you. If a person calls you to a vehicle, you do not need to go near the vehicle. Immediately inform parent, guardian or police.
*Be suspicious of any stranger asking for assistance.

* Be suspicious of a vehicle or person that seems out of place or a person who is watching you.

* Try to remember what the stranger looks like as well as the vehicle's licence plate number

* If a stranger asks you to help them find a pet, run away and inform parent, guardian, or nearest police officer (or park attendant). "say no, then go tell"

* Do not get into a car of a relative or neighbor without direct permission from parent or guardian.

* If a stranger approaches or follows you outside school, at the mall, or any public location, scream "stranger" and run to nearest responsible adult (Parent, guardian, teacher, police, firefighter, cashier, or security guard). If no responsible adult can be located, scream and run to a safe place (a neighbor, friend, or relatives home, a store, or anywhere, there is a crowd of people).

A safe place is usually not a wooded area, a pile of leaves, or an abandoned car or building.
* Do not go with a person who says your parents are in trouble or injured.

* When walking home from school, try to travel in groups. An abductor is least likely to approach a group and more likely to approach a child walking alone.

* Never take shortcuts through empty parks, fields, alleys

* Be assertive. You have the right to say "no" to anyone who tries to take you somewhere, touch you, or make you feel uncomfortable in any way.

Older Kids And Teenagers Should Also…

* Don't go jogging or running alone, late at night, or in a secluded or empty park. Try to run or jog with a partner despite the time of day.

* Never hitch hike.

* If attacked for money, jewelry or clothing, give it up rather than be injured.

* Inform parents if you are going to be late getting home after school. Explain to them the reason for lateness and where you will be.
* Talk to your parent when someone makes you feel uncomfortable or if someone touches you.

It is important to point out that a stranger is someone a child doesn't know, but that an abductor can be someone they are familiar with…someone they may trust. Therefore, it is important to be suspicious of any adult that acts in a way as depicted in the safety tips.

If a child becomes lost or separated from parents, the first reaction for a child is to wander around looking for them. This could possibly take the child further away and make them harder to find. What a child should do, is search out a responsible adult (cashier, security officer) and tell them that they have lost their parent(s) and need help.

Since most children refer to their parents as "mommy" and "daddy," make sure that child knows their full name, phone number and address as well as also how to write them. This way, "The parents of…" can be announced over the speaker or yelled into a crowd. If for some reason the parents happen to be

out of ear shot, a message could be left at the family home—
While the adult contacts the authority.

If a child is lost and there are no responsible adults around,
but there is a telephone, the child should know how to dial
"911" and await instructions.

If child is home alone and someone calls and asks to speak
to parent then child should always respond by saying that
their parents are busy. Afterwards, they should ask for a name
and phone number whereas the caller can be reached once
parents are available. If the household has caller I.D., then the
child should read phone number back to the caller, ask name,
and ask if this is the number parent should call once they
become available.

If a stranger knocks on the door, the child should move to
the rear of the home and not answer. If the door is forced open,
child should exit the rear of the home by door or window if
safely possible…then go scream for help. If there is no way to
safely exit a home due to living in an apartment, a child should
dial "911" and leave the phone of the hook, then lean out the
window and scream for help.

Obviously this is a lot of information to expect a child to
remember. That is why repetition is so important. The more
you repeat and reinforce the information, the more a child will
retain. Child therapist have said that a great way to help a child

retain information is to role play. Roll playing allows a child to visualize a situation instead of just listening to it. This can be achieved by performing little skits, by using puppets, or by using child's dolls and/or action figures. Instead of just describing the situation, try to explain it in the form of a story. To a child this will seem more like a family activity then a lesson. Older kids and teens may find roll playing to be lame, but do it anyway. Though focus more on discussions. Allow an older child to express their thoughts on the matter…don't just preach to them.

Whatever method you use, repeat and reinforce throughout childhood and teen years. Remember that a child could be abducted at any age. Don't allow yourself to believe that because your child is older, that they can protect themselves and that they are safe. There is always someone tougher and stronger. If you don't believe me, just look on the wall of your local post office and notice all the 15-19 year olds that go missing. We must believe that our children are vulnerable. That is the only way we can guarantee our resilience in the process of educating our children and ourselves.

Chapter Three

What Parents Should Know And Do To Keep Their Children Safe

A parent's responsibility doesn't end once a child has been taught safety tips and guidelines. That is just the beginning. This chapter will explore the importance of paying attention and listening to your children and also what a parent should know and do so to keep their children safe.

Here is a list of safety tips and guidelines for a parent, guardian, and nanny.

* Know where your children are at all times

* Never leave a small child alone at home, in a car, or in a stroller…not even for a moment.

* Make sure your child knows his or her full name, telephone number, and address.
* Create an environment where a child feels that they could talk to you.

* Always accompany your child on door to door activities such as Halloween—trick or treat-, school or youth organization fund raisers.

* Make sure that your children know where you work and that telephone number.

*Avoid putting a child's name on toys or clothing where the general public can see it. A predator may be looking for a child's name before approaching. A child is less likely to fear someone who knows his or her name.

* You should check all potential babysitters and older friends.

* Teach your children about strangers. Tell them never to talk to, take candy or gifts from, or go with a stranger without your direct consent.

* Make sure your child knows never to get into a stranger's vehicle.

* Tell your child that if they are approached by a stranger, run and scream and go tell.
* Point out safe houses (such as a friends home or a relatives home, a store, a church, a police station, or fire house) that your children can run to if in trouble.

* Let your children know that no one has the right to touch any part of his or her body that a bathing suit would cover.

* Inform your children to report to you, a police officer, or a school authority (security, teacher, Principle, coach, teachers' aide`) anyone who exposes his or her privates to them.

* Teach them that the police are their friends and that they can rely on them if they are in trouble.

* Report to police immediately, if your child informs you that they were lured or assaulted by a stranger, a family member, a neighbor, a teacher or a respected community member.

A parent must also be aware of child's routine and behavior patterns. If the routines and behavior patterns become inconsistent, then a parent or guardian should be on alert. Change could indicate something as simple as a new girlfriend or boyfriend or as complex and serious as drug usage or molestation. These changes could be the direct result of a child feeling embarrassed because they were touched inappropriately or because someone told them to keep a "special friendship" secret. This is when a parent or guardian really needs to pay attention to and listen to their child-clues may be revealed through their actions or what they say.

When I was in elementary school, I remember this one classmate that had this bizarre relation ship with one school aide. They would go to the movies and comic book conventions together and it was supposed to be this big secret. We all knew because this student would talk about it. None of us thought anything about it until one day he started acting strange. He told us that although he thought this teacher's aide was cool, He got tired of this guy showing up every where he was. At this time the whole relationship was making him feel uncomfortable. He continued to tell us that this guy was always touching him…not sexually or in any way as to imply sexuality…just gentle touches and caresses of the shoulder and neck.

At the age that we were, we couldn't see the potential threat their. Fortunately, one of the teachers did. This teacher ,noticing the change in the students behavior pulled him over to the side and questioned his home life. It turned out that the teacher suspected some kind of abuse at the family home. The teacher then called and requested that social services investigate. Social services interviewed the family and found them to be a loving family. The school aide, after hearing about the teachers action, never approached the child again. One year later this aide was arrested for allegedly sexually assaulting another student. This teacher could have protected this child from being molested or worst.

Knowing a child's, behavior patterns and being able to identify change could be the difference between keeping your child safe or a child getting abducted or being harmed by themselves or someone else. Change of behavior patterns and routines are something we as parents can't afford to ignore or dismiss.

Parks and Beaches

We all take our children to the park and to beaches so to bond with them. These moments can be precious, but only if we as parents and guardians participate. So many parents and guardians (and babysitters) bring children to these parks and beaches and send them to play while they read books or newspapers. In many cases a parent will come across another parent who had brought their child, and the two parents would begin to converse. Converse to the point that little if any attention is paid to the children, that is until a child begins to cry from falling or getting hurt or getting into a fight with another child.

It is those moments, whereas parents are completely engrossed in something other than their children, that these predators look for. Once again I must state that it only takes seconds to minutes to lure a child away. What a parent must do, is participate. Play with your children, roll around in the grass with them, climb on the jungle gym with them(if able), swim and splash with them. Two things will happen when you do this…Your child will be protected because a predator can't approach a child with the parent present, and two, your child will experience a kind of security and closeness that can only come from laughing and gigging and enjoying the company of a parent. Where the beach is concerned, not only does this protect a child from abduction, this could also protect your child from such dangers as drowning or exploring dangerous caverns and rock formations.

Chapter Four

Personal Identification Kits

What Is A Personal Identification Kit?

When a child is abducted or goes missing, it is a difficult time for the parents and family. Due to being upset and distraught it may be difficult and time consuming to gather the proper information. A Personal Identification Kit (more commonly known as an I.D. Kit) can provide biological information and photographs immediately. Immediate availability of this information will allow law enforcement to immediately institute an investigative action. Using this kit, a child's image and profile could be downloaded and available nation wide within minutes. The sooner an investigation begins, The better chance law enforcement have of returning a child home safely.

How To Make An Personal I.D. Kit

With the assistance of your local police department, any parent should be able to create an ID. kit of their children. Here's how...

First go to your local police department and have your child fingerprinted. In most regions police will do this as a free service and give you (the parent or guardian) the prints for your records. Some Police departments will also offer to photograph your child—also for your records. Since some will not supply photos, you must supply your own. Use the most recent pictures (at least two) that you can find. If you don't own a camera, find a inexpensive photo shop or mall photo booth. You can also buy an inexpensive disposable camera. Make sure photographs are as clear as possible. You should update photos every six months.

Next, purchase a pack of Q-Tips, a box of ziplock baggies, and a new comb or brush. Run the new comb or brush through child's hair several times and then place comb and brush with hair samples into a ziplock baggie-label, date, and seal. Then , take two Q-Tips out of the package (two Q-Tips per child). Rub one underneath or across child's tongue and rub second along the inside of child's mouth—against the inside of the cheek. Place those two saliva sample Q-Tips into a ziplock baggie, label, date and seal.

What you want next is a blood sample. This can usually be obtained from your local doctor, or a recently worn band-aides. Place these blood samples into a ziplock baggie, label, date and seal. You may also want to obtain child's dental record from child's dentist. Lastly place a handkerchief, shirt, sock, hat, or a piece of worn, but unwashed clothing into a baggie,(Item should have be worn for a full day and handled by no one other than that child) then label, date and seal. Once again—do not wash any of the items, because you want child's scent to be held on item so that a dog could use it to help in the tracking of missing child.

It is important that you make up a kit for each child in the home. Avoid cross contamination—each kit should be kept separate and placed next to each other in a safe place. Avoid placing kit one on top of each other if possible. If space dictates that you do place one on top of the other, than separate with plastic. Make sure you store kits in a location of accessability (a closet, a draw, a home safe). Do not store in post office or safety deposit box, or anywhere you must travel in order to retrieve it. Remember time is the enemy.

In the worst case scenario, this kit may help identify a young child's body and/or identify an abductor. The DNA and Fingerprints samples may be used to match DNA discovered in an abductors vehicle, house, or even on their clothing.

Chapter Five

The Internet

In the technological age in which we live, The introduction of the Internet was a blessing and a curse. No more hours spent in the library doing homework and research, Now everything one needed was simply at their fingertips. The Internet also opened up a whole new world to the child predator. When once these predators lurked in the shadows looking for an innocent child, now all they have to do is enter a chat room and communicate directly with a host of would be victims. It has become just like fishing…drop the bait and wait for someone to bite.

Some predators have pretended to be children and teens and act as a chat and pen pal. Others have pretended to be royalty, musicians and rappers, or heir to family fortunes. They promise the would be victim the world and when the time is right, these predators set up a meeting. Often they make meeting so desirable that the child initiates it. Some abductor, simply look for a child or teen who has just discovered their sexuality and are looking for a secret way to explore it. The predator will listen to and then become the personification of youths fantasy. In some cases they even supply photographs of some one they feel will be attractive to their prey. Once a child or teen is enticed enough, a meeting may be arranged. In a lot of these situations the child is likely to do all the sneaking around. All the a predator needs to do is sit back and wait for child or teen to arrive and they got them. A parent may never even be aware that their child had been communicating with a stranger.

So how do we protect our children from the dangers that lurk online? Well, lets start with the location of the family computer. I have always been against a child having a computer in their room. I believe that this gives a child too much privacy and too much accessability to the computer at all hours of the night. I prefer to have a family computer out in the open where the computer can be supervised. It is more difficult, not impossible, for a child to communicate with someone in secret if the whole family can see what you are doing. Don't get me wrong…I'm not saying hang over your teens shoulder as they E-mail friends and invade their privacy, I mean let them know that you are paying attention and that you have a right to know who they are communicating with. Just feeling your presence may be all that is needed the dissuade a child from communicating with someone they know they shouldn't.

Unfortunately, many children do have computers in their bedrooms or in a secluded room down the hall or in the basement. In a situation like this a child can be undisturbed and unobserved as they surf the net. In order to secure your children safety you should follow these guidelines…

* Get informed about computers and the Internet.

* Create simple and easy to read house rule and post them along side the key board or on the computer near the monitor. Rules should be periodically reviewed and discussed.

* Most online servers have existing safeguarding programs that you can take advantage of. Some of these include monitoring and filtering. Ask about these safeguards and how to use them to the fullest.

*Always read a websites privacy policy before giving any personal information. Also, make sure that a website offers a secure connection before giving credit cards.

* A child should never order anything online without parents direct involvement…even if its "free".

* If your child uses chatrooms or e-mail, talk to your child about never meeting a stranger or online friend face to face. Explain that even if they had been talking to each other for some time, that person met on line is still a stranger.

* Talk to your child about responding to offensive and/or dangerous e-mail, chat, or other communications. Report any such communication to local law enforcement immediately.

* Keep the computer in an open area or family room. Make sure this family room is not in an attic, basement, or secluded location of the home.

* Let your children show you what they can do online and visit their favorite web sites and/or chatrooms.

*Have your children use child friendly search engines when doing homework. (You can find a list of child friendly search engines at the rear of this book).

*If you suspect online stalking or sexual exploitation of a child, report it to your local law enforcement immediately.

*The National Center For Missing & Exploited Children (NCMEC) has a system for identifying online predators and children pornographers called the "Cyber Tipline." Visit www.netsmartzz.org/parents.

* Know who your children are exchanging e-mail and instant messages with, and only let them use chat areas that you have visited and approve of. Limit chatroom access to child friendly sites for children in the proper age group.

* As child uses chatroom, spot check what they are talking about. (Remember that an adult could be lurking about in the disguise of a child.)

*Be aware of any other computers that your child may be using. (Most libraries no longer have child protection, monitoring, or filtering).

* Internet accounts should be in parents name with parents having the primary screen name, controlling password, and using blocking and/or filtering devices.

* Children should not complete a profile for an online service provider and children's screen names should be non-descript so as not to identify that the user is a child.

Following these guidelines will allow your child to have a more enjoyable computer experience while giving you peace of mind. But don't let piece of mind take you off your game. You must always be on the job.

Chapter Six

What To Do If Child Is Abducted Or Goes Missing

If your child is abducted or goes missing, the first thing you want to do is stay calm and call 911, then follow these guidelines.

* Call the FBI (phone number can be found in the rear of book).

* Call local sheriff's office

* Call your local radio station and inform them that your child is missing.

*Call your local television station and inform them that your child is missing.

* Call child locator services (see rear of this book)

* Call The National Center for Missing & Exploited Children (NCMEC)-1(800) 843-5678. Ask NCMEC to contact the FBI child abduction and serial killer unit as to whether or not their services would be appropriate.

* Make sure child is registered in FBI NCIC computer as "stranger abducted" if you believe this to be the case.

* When law enforcement arrives, immediately supply them with all pertinent information and hand them the personal identification kit of that child.

* Try to remember and write down the exact outfit that your child was wearing.

* In giving law enforcement a description of child, be as thorough as possible. Mention any scars, birthmarks, bruises, tatoos, or piercings.

* Point out any identifying facts of your child. (Has asthma, speaks several different language, blinks often, favorite standing position, nail bitter, etc).
* Make a list of all friends, teachers, coaches and neighbors that your child had spent some time with.

* Write down place the your child routinely visits.

* Examine children room, but don't move anything. This room has become a crime scene and trained investigators need to find it as it was left by missing child.
Clues may be revealed in this room—especially if child had gone to meet a "stranger" or "secret friend.:"

* If child has a diary or journal, turn it over to law enforcement immediately. If the diary exist, but you don't know where it is, inform law enforcement of its existence.

* If you don't already have caller i.d. , install it into your phone system. (In case abductor of child contacts you).

* If you can obtain a recording device, connect it to your phone. (In case abductors contact you). Ask your local law enforcement if they have device.

* Follow all instructions and cooperate completely with law enforcement

As stated in chapter four, the more information you can supply and the faster you make it available, the faster and more thorough law enforcement can do their jobs, the faster the Amber alert plan can be initiated (see chapter 8). Once again, time is of the essence. The sooner an investigation begins, the better chance of a child being returned home safely.

Distribution of Flyers

When planning to distribute flyers, gather up-to-date photos (at least two). If you don't have photo's, pictures can be obtained from recent videos. Write down all pertinent information to describe missing child. With this task done, choose a location to meet volunteers. A local copy shop is a great choice because as soon as flyers are printed , you and your group will be ready to go. Other suggestion are local churches, community center, schools, local library, and local police station. Try to obtain police assistance and try to check out all volunteers. Let law enforcement lead. Even though law enforcement will fax flyers to the media, do it yourself. Fax flyers to television stations, radio stations, and cable systems. Distribute flyers to as many locations as possible. Make sure you get permission before posting. You don't want property owner removing flyers out of anger without reading them.

If any of the volunteer have a problem posting flyers in stores and shops, call those stores and shops yourself. People find it difficult to reject a distraught parent.

If 48 hour has past and child is still missing, use your imagination to keep the public aware of your plight. Here are some things you can do.

* Ask local post office if delivery people could insert flyers into mail boxes on their route.

* Ask local pizza shop owners and Chinese restaurant to attach flyers to all deliveries.

* put flyers into every letter, bill, and package that you mail.

* Try to book interviews with newspapers, radio programs, and television and cable programs.

* Ask motorcycle clubs, veterans, and other clubs to distribute flyers.

The more people that know of your missing child, the better chance of child being recognized.

Rewards

Offering rewards are a tricky practice. In some cases it may be what is needed to motivate an abductor to return a child or to get the assistance of volunteers. Before you offer a reward, talk to your lawyer. If you do not have a lawyer , hire one and ask them if they will work "Pro Bono" (that means at no cost to you.) You should also discuss this with law enforcement. Don't be surprised if law enforcement gives you a hard time about offering a reward. Rewards can sometime create many false leads that can hamper and slow down the investigation.

Another thing that you should consider is that if a reward is offered , its like a signed contract. If some one complies as per your request, you must pay. You are making a legal agreement to pay an amount to anyone entitled to claim rewards including abductors. You can be sued for the full amount if you don't keep promise as stated. Also if worded poorly, many people can become entitled and eligible to claim reward. That is why you must make sure a lawyer assist you in the wording and legalities before reward is offered.

Donations

Other than using ones own money, ask for donation to assist you in bringing your missing child home. As donations start to come in, set up a separate account just for received donations. Do not deposit donations into your personal bank account. You also want to avoid having direct contact with any funds you receive. Appoint someone trust worth to manage it.
Here are some other important suggestions you should remember:

* Be prepared for accusation concerning use of donation. Make sure accurate spending records are kept. (The public is always looking for a scandal even in the midst of your pain).
* Be honest, the public should know how the money will be used.

* Never reveal to the media the number of donations or the amount of donations.

If any funds go unused for whatever reason, return donations to person or organizations if possible. If not possible, donate funds to a missing children's organization of your choice.

Estranged Parent

When a child of a single parent vanishes or goes missing, one must automatically consider estranged parents to be a suspect. Supply law enforcement with all the information you could think of. Their name and any aliases that they might use, where they live, where they hangout, friends, girlfriends or boyfriends, parents and sibling information and where they live, type of vehicle driven by them. Type of vehicle driven by girlfriends/boyfriends and license plate numbers if you know them.

If you believe that they may attempt to leave the country, call all airports in your and neighboring states. Inform law enforcement immediately. Fax them a picture of child and parent. It is very difficult to retrieve a child once they have escaped the country, so do everything in your power to make it impossible for them to get out. When you have done everything in your power to keep them grounded, then treat it as any other abduction. Do not assume that the missing child won't be harmed because they were abducted by a parent. Odds are the parent won't harm the child, but that's not a chance you should want to take. Treat the situation as if anything is possible.

Chapter Seven

How A Child Can Fight Back If Abducted

What you're about to read may seem harsh, but under the circumstance it must be stated. If a child is kidnaped by a stranger, they are most like going to die unless they can escape the situation. They can't just assume that all will turn out okay. Due to the severity of the situation, they must scream, kick, bite, and scratch, and do what ever it takes…as if their lives depend on it, because most likely it does.

In this chapter we are going to explore different ideas on how to fight back and escape when abduction.

When Grabbed

When grabbed by an abductor, child should scream as loud as they can, "fire", "this is not my parent", "help", and/or "stranger". They should keep on screaming, even if abductor has a weapons. The abducted child hasn't served their purpose at this time so harming them at this point is unlikely. The child needs to draw as much attention to themselves as possible. Enough that child may be released or gain the assistance of bystanders. Child should also kick (in the groin if possible. The knee and shin are also suggested targets). They should bite whatever and where ever they can on the abductors body. Attempts at poking eyes and scratching abductors face are suggested and if they can get close enough, push hard on the tip of abductors nose. (In and upward). If child gets free, they should run to the most crowded area as possible. (A store, bank, library, the middle of a street, nearest house, etc.) All the while still screaming. If they are grabbed from behind, they should drop and twist and run away screaming. If they are grabbed by the wrist, they should pull down and push back on abductors thumb or bite them on the wrist as hard as possible.

If Placed In a Trunk of Car

If placed in the trunk of a car, child should wait until car starts moving then attempt to kick out rear headlights. A missing headlight may draw the attention of the police or another driver. If they can, they should stick their hand through hole and wave for help. Parent should inform law enforcement that child knows how to kick out rear lights, so that they can stop all vehicles without rear light. Another thing they can do is rip up the carpeting and then yank on any wires the can find. This may cause the rear light to flicker and draw attention to the vehicle. If the police pull the car over, when the vehicle comes to a stop, scream if you can and/or kick against the trunk. Most of the new cars, however, have a release that will open the trunk make sure your child knows what it looks like. You may have to take your child to a car dealer ship to do that.

If Placed Inside Vehicle

If placed inside a vehicle, they should climb to the back seat so they can get the back door open and escape. If car is moving, when it comes to a stoplight or slows down they should try to open door. If door is locked and window can't be opened, attempt to kick out window and escape. They should not worry about being hurt or getting cut after jumping from moving vehicle, it's better than the alternative. Using ones hand, blind fold abductor or driver (as if playing "guess who"). A few seconds of driving blind may attract the attention of another driver or police. If in the front of vehicle, they should drop down and reach under dashboard and rip out any wires they can find. This will usually cause the vehicle not to start or to stop if already moving. They can also gain attention if child can force drivers foot on the accelerator or break and cause dramatic changes of speed. Grabbing the steering wheel may work also as will pounding on the horn.

If In A Store Or Parking Lot

If in a store, child should knock things off the shelve so to attract attention to themselves. They should use their eyes to communicate that they are in danger. They also could Fall to the floor of the store and scream as loud as possible.

While in a parking garage, they should run and slam into cars and attempt to set off alarms. They should try pulling on car doors also, this may be what sets off some alarm.

If Inside a House or Hotel

If a child is held captive inside a house they should stay alert and keep their eyes open for an opportunity for escape. If possible, they should flash the lights of the room in a :SOS formation. When getting tied up child should tighten wrist and inflate chest as much as possible and hold it until they are alone enough to relax. this will make the rope/tape/handcuffs looser when in a relaxed mode. It may make escaping the ropes/tape/handcuffs possible. If they think they can make it to a door or window without being caught, they should go for it.

Leaving a Trail

Leaving a trail is very important. One thing a child can do is to drop their necklace, bracelet or any identifying object out a car window or at a public bathroom. If they have the means to write little notes, they should do so and drop them where ever you go. Try to use the bathroom as often as possible, once inside look for a way out or a way to leave a clue. Leave a hat or a pair of socks behind. This will leave a fresh scent for dog to follow as well as inform police of where abouts or direction traveling. Child should touch as many things as possible so to leave fingerprint. Child should try to leave a lasting impression with clerks, patrons, and security.

I have found that playing "secret agent" is a good way of teaching these technics without traumatizing a child. You want them to understand that these things could be done in the real world. Briefly discuss how these technics work against would be abductors, and let them climb inside a car and make believe they are using technic they have learned, then go back to playing the game. Make it all about the game. The child will learn as they laugh and play with the people that make them feel secure…you the parents/guardian.

Chapter Eight

The Amber Alert System

In 1996, 9 year old Amber Hagerman was kidnaped and brutally murdered in Arlington Texas. The tragedy so upset and outraged the entire community that residents contacted radio stations in the Dallas area and suggested the broadcasting of special "alerts" over the airwaves. These "alerts", it was believed, could help prevent such future incidents. The Dallas/Fort Worth Association of Radio Managers teamed up with local law enforcement in northern Texas and developed this innovative early warning system to help to find abducted children in direct response to the community's concern for the safety of local children.

This is how it works...

Once law enforcement has been contacted and notified of an abducted child, they must first determine if the case meets the amber plans criteria for sounding off an alert. Each program establishes it's own AMBER Plan criteria, however, the National Center for missing and exploited children (NCMEC.)

Suggest three criteria that should be met before an alert is sounded.

* Law enforcement confirms a child has been abducted.

* Law enforcement believes the circumstances surrounding the abduction indicate that the child is in danger of serious bodily harm or death.

*There is enough descriptive information about the child, abductor, and or suspects vehicle to believe an immediate broadcast alert will help.

If these criteria are met, alert information must be put together for public distribution. This information can include description, pictures of missing child, the suspected abductor, a suspected vehicle and any other information available and valuable to identifying the child and suspect.

The information is then faxed to radio stations designated as primary stations under the Emergency Alert Systems (EAS). These primary stations send the same information to area radio and television stations and cable systems via the EAS, and it is immediately broadcast by participating stations to millions of listeners. Radio stations interrupt programming to announce the alert, and television stations and cable systems run a "crawl" on the screen along with a picture of the child.

(Information courtesy of The National Center For Missing & Exploited Children)

This system has been tremendously successful. So much so that it is being adopted in several regions and states. It is even being adopted into some regions of Canada.

* The AMBER Alert Plan has been credited with the recovery of several children—over 26 at time of this books publishing.

Conclusion

There has been a lot of information supplied to you in this book, so take your time and absorb it. I personally suggest the one reads this book in it's entirety then take notes during and immediate reread. I have even supplied a section for notes in the rear of this book.

From The Author

I truly pray that you and your children may never have to live through the nightmares and horrors described herein, but with so many children abducted and attacked in this country every year, the chances are great that your lives will be touched, directly if not indirectly, by these sick and twisted individuals that prey on the young and weak. To borrow a phrase from the ABC television educational program "School House Rock",…"Knowledge is power"and I challenge you to weld that power like a sword. Don't believe that it can't happen to your family, make it so that if it does you and your children will be prepared. Let's use knowledge and preparation to strike back so that we may watch all our children grow-up and reach their full potential.

For your conviennience in the case of an emergency, I have supplied you with the following:

* A list of national missing children organizations

* A list of international missing children organizations

* A list of emergency hot lines and help lines

* A list of child safe Internet search engines

* Other recommended books

* Child Personal I.D. Kit worksheet

* A place to keep notes

List Of National Missing Children Organizations

NATIONAL CENTER FOR MISSING & EXPLOITED
CHILDREN
(NCMEC)
1-(800) THE-LOST or 1-(800) 843-5678

NCMEC BRANCH OFFICES
CALIFORNIA (714) 508-0150
FLORIDA (561) 848-1900
KANSAS CITY (816) 361-4554
NEW YORK (716) 242-0900
SOUTH CAROLINA (803) 254-2326

ARIZONA
The Nation's Missing Children Organization
and Center for Missing Adults
(800) 690-FIND
CONNECTICUT
The Paul and Lisa Program
(860) 767-7660

FLORIDA
Missing Children Help Center
(800) USA-KIDS

GEORGIA
Children's Rights of America, Inc.
(800) 442-HOPE

MICHIGAN
Missing Children's Network of Michigan
(800) 98-KATHY

MINNESOTA
The JacobWetterling Foundation
(800) 325-HOPE
Missing Children-Minnesota
(888) RUN-YELL

NEBRASKA
Missing Youth Foundation
(800) 52-FOUND

NEVADA
Nevada Child Seekers
(702) 458-7009

OREGON
National Missing Children's Locate Center
(503) 257-1308
(800) 999-7846 (sightings)

TENNESSEE
Commission on Missing and Exploited Children (COMEC)
(901) 528-8441

TEXAS
Child Search—National Missing Children Center
(800) 832-3773
Heidi Search Center, Inc.
(210) 650-0428

WASHINGTON
Operation Lookout/National Center for Missing Youth
(800) 782-7335 (USA)
(800) LOOKOUT x 1234 (International)

CANADA
Child Find Canada
(800) 387-7962
Missing Children Society of Canada
(800) 661-6160
The Missing Children's Network/Le Reseau Enfants Retour Canada
(514) 843-4333

List Of International Missing Children Organizations

Association Para la Recuperasion de Ninos Sacados de su Pais:
Spain
Telephone: (34) 97 62 16 613 Fax: (34) 97 62 38 500

Collectif de Soliarite aux Meres des Enfants Enleves Meres
d'alger: France
Telephone: 33-145 344 910 Fax:33-146-231-164

Comite Francais cotreLes Enlevements Parentaux D'Enfants:
France
Telephone: (33)1 39 70 88 99 Fax: (33) 1 39 74 20 5

Commitee for Missing Children/Europe Germany
Telephone: 49(0) 6184902

Empty Arms Network: Ausralia
Telephone: 61(3) 98 82 55 43 Fax: 61 (3) 98 83 55 22

Irish Center for Parentally Abducted Children: IRELAND
Telephone: 353 1 6620667 Fax: 353 1 6625132

Missing Children International Network: elgium
Telephone: (32) (0) 84-21-1461 Fax: (32) (0) 84-22-1394

Kinderschutz International e. V. Germany
Telephone: 49-221-121-616

List Of Emergency Hotline And Help Lines

NATIONAL CENTER FOR MISSING & EXPLOITED
CHILDREN
1-800-THE-LOST (1-800-843-5678)

CYBER TIPLINE
WWW.MISSINGKIDS.COM/CYBERTIP
1-800-843-5678

NATIONAL RUNAWAY HOTLINE
1-800-231-6946

NATIONAL RUNAWAY SWITCHBOARD
A Messaging service to help parents and runaway communicate.
1-800-621-4000

TEAM HOPE
Parent network for families of missing children offering
encouragement, support
1-800-306-3611

List Of Child Safe Search Engines

Ask Jeeves for kids
Yahooligans
Lycos SafetyNet
OneKey
Education World
Classroom Connection
Study Web
KidsClick
Disney Dig Internet Guide
WebCrawler Kids and Family Channel

Other Recommended Books

THE RECOVERY OF INTERNATIONAL CHILDREN:
A COMPREHENSIVE GUIDE
By Maureen Dabbagh
When a child is abducted and taken out of the country by a parent, the enormous task of coordinating a recovery effort is the custodian parents responsibility. To make that task more manageable, Dabbagh has compiled this guide. Outlining the legal process step by step describing the many people and agencies involved, and telling how to help them work together.

*

THE PARENT'S GUIDE TO PROTECTING YOUR
CHILD
IN CYBERSPACE
By Parry Aftab
An in depth look at the dangers a child faces while surfing the internet. A very powerful and thorough guide on how to keep them safe and give you piece of mind.

Personal i.d. Kit worksheet

About You (Parent Or Guardian)

Name: Last_____ First_____ MI_____
Date of Birth ___/___/___ Relationship to child _____
Street Address_____
City_____ State/Zip code_____
Telephone #/Home_____ Business_____

About Your Child

Name: Last_____ First_____ MI_____
Nickname_____ Social Security_____
Date of Birth_____/_____/_____   Gender (Sex) Male___
Female___
Place of Birth (Municipality/State/ County)_____
_____

Race:
Black__ White__ American Indian/Alaskan Native__
Hispanic__ Asian__ Other__

As your child grows, take his or her measurements at least once
each year and record them below:

Date_____/_____/_____ Height(HGT)_____(Ft/in)
         Weight(WGT)_____

Date_____/_____/_____ Height(HGT)_____(Ft/in)
         Weight(WGT)_____

Date_____/_____/_____ Height(HGT)_____(Ft/in)
         Weight(WGT)_____

Date_____/_____/_____ Height(HGT)_____(Ft/in)
         Weight(WGT)_____

Date_____/_____/_____ Height(HGT)_____(Ft/in)
         Weight(WGT)_____

Date_____/_____/_____ Height(HGT)_____(Ft/in)
         Weight(WGT)_____

Date_____/_____/_____ Height(HGT)_____(Ft/in)
         Weight(WGT)_____

Date_____/_____/_____ Height(HGT)_____(Ft/in)
         Weight(WGT)_____

Date_____/_____/_____ Height(HGT)_____(Ft/in)
         Weight(WGT)_____

Date_____/_____/_____ Height(HGT)_____(Ft/in)
         Weight(WGT)_____

Date_____/_____/_____ Height(HGT)_____(Ft/in)
         Weight(WGT)_____

Date_____/_____/_____ Height(HGT)_____(Ft/in)
         Weight(WGT)_____

Date_____/_____/_____ Height(HGT)_____(Ft/in)
         Weight(WGT)_____

Date_____/_____/_____ Height(HGT)_____(Ft/in)
                 Weight(WGT)_____
Date_____/_____/_____ Height(HGT)_____(Ft/in)
                 Weight(WGT)_____
Date_____/_____/_____ Height(HGT)_____(Ft/in)
                 Weight(WGT)_____

Eye Color__   Hair Color__   Skin Complexion_
Blood Type__   Foot Size____   Glasses: Yes_ No_
Contacts:Yes_ No_ Circumcision:Yes_ No_ Braces: Yes_ No_

Scars, Marks, Birth Marks, Tattoos, Piercing or Brands—
Describe and include locations:_____
_____
_____
_____

Medical Conditions and Required Medications: _____
_____
_____
_____

Commonly Worn Jewelry Type and Location of jewelry: ____
_____
_____
_____

School Name and Address: _____
_____

Mother's Name (Including Maiden) and Father's Name _____
_____

Physician: Name, Office Address and Telephone #: _____

_____

Dentist: Name, Office Address, Telephone #: _____

_____

Other Notes _____

_____

_____

_____

_____

_____

_____

_____

_____

_____

Personal i.d. Kit worksheet

About You (Parent Or Guardian)

Name: Last_____ First_____ MI_____
Date of Birth ___/___/___ Relationship to child _____
Street Address_____
City_____ State/Zip code_____
Telephone #/Home_____ Business_____

About Your Child

Name: Last_____ First_____ MI_____
Nickname_____ Social Security_____
Date of Birth_____/_____/_____ Gender (Sex) Male___
Female___
Place of Birth (Municipality/State/ County)_____

Race:
Black__ White__ American Indian/Alaskan Native__
Hispanic__ Asian__ Other__
As your child grows, take his or her measurements at least once
each year and record them below:

Date_____/_____/_____ Height(HGT)_____(Ft/in)
                  Weight(WGT)_____

Date_____/_____/_____ Height(HGT)_____(Ft/in)
                  Weight(WGT)_____

Date_____/_____/_____ Height(HGT)_____(Ft/in)
                  Weight(WGT)_____

Date_____/_____/_____ Height(HGT)_____(Ft/in)
                  Weight(WGT)_____

Date_____/_____/_____ Height(HGT)_____(Ft/in)
                  Weight(WGT)_____

Date_____/_____/_____ Height(HGT)_____(Ft/in)
                  Weight(WGT)_____

Date_____/_____/_____ Height(HGT)_____(Ft/in)
                  Weight(WGT)_____

Date_____/_____/_____ Height(HGT)_____(Ft/in)
                  Weight(WGT)_____

Date_____/_____/_____ Height(HGT)_____(Ft/in)
                  Weight(WGT)_____

Date_____/_____/_____ Height(HGT)_____(Ft/in)
                  Weight(WGT)_____

Date_____/_____/_____ Height(HGT)_____(Ft/in)
                  Weight(WGT)_____

Date_____/_____/_____ Height(HGT)_____(Ft/in)
                  Weight(WGT)_____

Date_____/_____/_____ Height(HGT)_____(Ft/in)
                  Weight(WGT)_____

Date_____/_____/_____ Height(HGT)_____(Ft/in)
Weight(WGT)_____
Date_____/_____/_____ Height(HGT)_____(Ft/in)
Weight(WGT)_____
Date_____/_____/_____ Height(HGT)_____(Ft/in)
Weight(WGT)_____

Eye Color__   Hair Color__   Skin Complexion_
Blood Type__   Foot Size____   Glasses: Yes_ No_
Contacts:Yes_ No_ Circumcision:Yes_ No_ Braces: Yes_ No_

Scars, Marks, Birth Marks, Tattoos, Piercing or Brands—
Describe and include locations:_____

_____

_____

Medical Conditions and Required Medications: _____

_____

_____

Commonly Worn Jewelry Type and Location of jewelry: ____

_____

_____

School Name and Address: _____

_____

Mother's Name (Including Maiden) and Father's Name _____

_____

Physician: Name, Office Address and Telephone #: _____

_____

_____

Dentist: Name, Office Address, Telephone #: _____

_____

_____

Other Notes _____

_____

_____

_____

_____

_____

_____

_____

_____

_____

Personal i.d. Kit worksheet

About You (Parent Or Guardian)

Name: Last_____ First_____ MI_____

Date of Birth ___/___/___ Relationship to child _____

Street Address_____

City_____ State/Zip code_____

Telephone #/Home_____ Business_____

About Your Child

Name: Last_____ First_____ MI_____

Nickname_____ Social Security_____

Date of Birth_____/_____/_____   Gender (Sex) Male___

Female___

Place of Birth (Municipality/State/ County)_____

_____

Race:

Black__ White__ American Indian/Alaskan Native__
Hispanic__ Asian__ Other__

As your child grows, take his or her measurements at least once
each year and record them below:

Date_____/_____/_____ Height(HGT)_____(Ft/in)
                Weight(WGT)_____

Date_____/_____/_____ Height(HGT)_____(Ft/in)
                Weight(WGT)_____

Date_____/_____/_____ Height(HGT)_____(Ft/in)
                Weight(WGT)_____

Date_____/_____/_____ Height(HGT)_____(Ft/in)
                Weight(WGT)_____

Date_____/_____/_____ Height(HGT)_____(Ft/in)
                Weight(WGT)_____

Date_____/_____/_____ Height(HGT)_____(Ft/in)
                Weight(WGT)_____

Date_____/_____/_____ Height(HGT)_____(Ft/in)
                Weight(WGT)_____

Date_____/_____/_____ Height(HGT)_____(Ft/in)
                Weight(WGT)_____

Date_____/_____/_____ Height(HGT)_____(Ft/in)
                Weight(WGT)_____

Date_____/_____/_____ Height(HGT)_____(Ft/in)
                Weight(WGT)_____

Date_____/_____/_____ Height(HGT)_____(Ft/in)
                Weight(WGT)_____

Date_____/_____/_____ Height(HGT)_____(Ft/in)
                Weight(WGT)_____

Date_____/_____/_____ Height(HGT)_____(Ft/in)
                Weight(WGT)_____

Date_____/_____/_____ Height(HGT)_____(Ft/in)
                        Weight(WGT)_____
Date_____/_____/_____ Height(HGT)_____(Ft/in)
                        Weight(WGT)_____
Date_____/_____/_____ Height(HGT)_____(Ft/in)
                        Weight(WGT)_____

Eye Color__   Hair Color__   Skin Complexion_
Blood Type__   Foot Size____   Glasses: Yes_ No_
Contacts:Yes_ No_ Circumcision:Yes_ No_Braces: Yes_ No_

Scars, Marks, Birth Marks, Tattoos, Piercing or Brands—
Describe and include locations:_____
_____
_____
_____

Medical Conditions and Required Medications: _____
_____
_____
_____

Commonly Worn Jewelry Type and Location of jewelry: ____
_____
_____
_____

School Name and Address: _____
_____

Mother's Name (Including Maiden) and Father's Name _____
_____

Physician: Name, Office Address and Telephone #: _____

_____

_____

Dentist: Name, Office Address, Telephone #: _____

_____

_____

Other Notes _____

_____

_____

_____

_____

_____

_____

_____

_____

_____

Personal i.d. Kit worksheet

About You (Parent Or Guardian)

Name: Last_____ First_____ MI_____

Date of Birth ___/___/___ Relationship to child _____

Street Address_____

City_____ State/Zip code_____

Telephone #/Home_____ Business_____

About Your Child

Name: Last_____ First_____ MI_____

Nickname_____ Social Security_____

Date of Birth_____/_____/_____   Gender (Sex) Male___

Female___

Place of Birth (Municipality/State/ County)_____

_____

Race:

Black__ White__ American Indian/Alaskan Native__

Hispanic__ Asian__ Other__

As your child grows, take his or her measurements at least once each year and record them below:

Date_____/_____/_____   Height(HGT)_____(Ft/in)
                  Weight(WGT)_____
Date_____/_____/_____   Height(HGT)_____(Ft/in)
                  Weight(WGT)_____
Date_____/_____/_____   Height(HGT)_____(Ft/in)
                  Weight(WGT)_____
Date_____/_____/_____   Height(HGT)_____(Ft/in)
                  Weight(WGT)_____
Date_____/_____/_____   Height(HGT)_____(Ft/in)
                  Weight(WGT)_____
Date_____/_____/_____   Height(HGT)_____(Ft/in)
                  Weight(WGT)_____
Date_____/_____/_____   Height(HGT)_____(Ft/in)
                  Weight(WGT)_____
Date_____/_____/_____   Height(HGT)_____(Ft/in)
                  Weight(WGT)_____
Date_____/_____/_____   Height(HGT)_____(Ft/in)
                  Weight(WGT)_____
Date_____/_____/_____   Height(HGT)_____(Ft/in)
                  Weight(WGT)_____
Date_____/_____/_____   Height(HGT)_____(Ft/in)
                  Weight(WGT)_____
Date_____/_____/_____   Height(HGT)_____(Ft/in)
                  Weight(WGT)_____
Date_____/_____/_____   Height(HGT)_____(Ft/in)
                  Weight(WGT)_____

Date_____/_____/_____ Height(HGT)_____(Ft/in)
                    Weight(WGT)_____
Date_____/_____/_____ Height(HGT)_____(Ft/in)
                    Weight(WGT)_____
Date_____/_____/_____ Height(HGT)_____(Ft/in)
                    Weight(WGT)_____

Eye Color__   Hair Color__   Skin Complexion_
Blood Type__   Foot Size_____   Glasses: Yes_ No_
Contacts:Yes_ No_ Circumcision:Yes_ No_ Braces: Yes_ No_

Scars, Marks, Birth Marks, Tattoos, Piercing or Brands—
Describe and include locations:_____
_____
_____
_____

Medical Conditions and Required Medications: _____
_____
_____
_____

Commonly Worn Jewelry Type and Location of jewelry: ____
_____
_____
_____

School Name and Address: _____
_____
Mother's Name (Including Maiden) and Father's Name _____
_____

Physician: Name, Office Address and Telephone #: _____

_____

_____

Dentist: Name, Office Address, Telephone #: _____

_____

_____

Other Notes _____

_____

_____

_____

_____

_____

_____

_____

_____

_____

_____

About the Author

Maurice Woodson began writing professionally while still in high school when he published a small socially conscience magazine out of his family's Bronx N.Y. apartment. He then contributed to several national magazines and local newspapers. He has authored three children's books (soon to be released) and has published A book on pregnancy and childbirth. As a volunteer to several youth and family organizations, he has made family appreciation and togetherness his mission.

Maurice Woodson is a father of three and currently lives in New York State.

Notes

Notes

Notes

Notes

Notes

Notes

Notes

Notes

Notes

Notes

Notes

Notes

Notes

0-595-25360-1